Green Box Kids Learn About Flexibility

A comic book-based social skills curriculum

Written by:
Carl Dzyak, M.Ed., BCBA, LBA
Barbara Kaminski, Ph.D., BCBA-D, LBA
Christopher Richardson, M.Ed., BCBA, LBA

Illustrated by:
Sarah Miller

Copyright ©2016 Green Box ABA, PLLC
All Rights Reserved by, and remain the intellectual property of, the Author.

This book is for individual or classroom use only. This product contains copyrighted text and graphics. Except as permitted under the Copyright Act of 1976, no part of this book may be reproduced in any form or by any electronic or mechanical means, including the use of information storage and retrieval systems, without permission in writing from the copyright owner. Requests for permissions should be addressed in writing to Green Box ABA, PLLC, Attn: Carl Dzyak, 6216 Old Keene Mill Court, Springfield, VA 22152

This is a work of fiction. Names, characters, businesses, places, events and incidents are either the products of the author's imagination or used in a fictitious manner. Any resemblance to actual persons, living or dead, or actual events is purely coincidental.

This book is not intended as a substitute for the medical advice of physicians. The reader should regularly consult a physician in matters relating to his/her health and particularly with respect to any symptoms that may require diagnosis or medical attention.

www.greenboxABA.org

www.facebook.com/GreenBoxABA

www.twitter.com/GreenBoxEdu

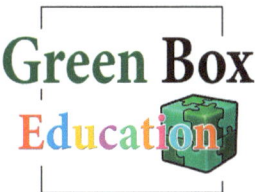

This book is dedicated to the cool kids who do the awesome things that inspire us every day.

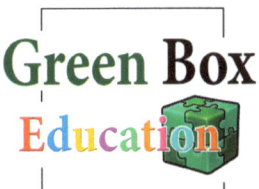

Table of Contents

Welcome to the Green Box Social Skills Curriculum!..................1
  Social Skills Are Foundational! 1
  What Is Applied Behavior Analysis?..................2
  Overview of The Green Box Kids Social Skills Curriculum 2
  About This Volume..................4
  How To Use This Book..................4
  How To Measure Progress..................5
  Summary and Extension..................6

Lesson 1: Traffic..................7
  Let's Break It Down! 10
  Let's Think About It!..................17
  Let's See What We Learned! 23
  Let's See What The Green Box Kids Came Up With!..................26

Lesson 2: The Party..................29
  Let's Break It Down! 32
  Let's Think About It!..................39
  Let's See What We Learned! 45
  Let's See What The Green Box Kids Came Up With!..................48

Lesson 3: The Test..................51
  Let's Break It Down! 54
  Let's Think About It..................61
  Let's See What We Learned! 68
  Let's See What The Green Box Kids Came Up With!..................71

Appendix A: Measuring Progress..................75
Appendix B: Individualized Education Program Goals..................81
Appendix C: For the ABA Professional..................83

Introduction

Welcome To The Green Box Social Skills Curriculum!

Each volume of the curriculum concentrates on a specific social skill that may present a challenge, particularly for a child with special needs. Each of the three lessons in every volume consists of a comic and activities. The comics feature the Green Box Kids in challenging social scenarios. The interactions are presented with minimal text in a child-friendly, visually-striking format to help engage the student in the social lesson with ease and enjoyment.

Social Skills Are Foundational!

Family. School. Neighborhoods. Sports Teams. Clubs. The enjoyment and success of participating in such social groups is related, in many ways, to the ability to function in social settings. Given the amount of time spent in social groups, both as a child and into adulthood, learning social skills is a vital component of a child's overall development.

Social Skills Impairments in Children with Special Needs

While all children sometimes experience difficulties navigating complicated social situations, the child with special needs often needs extra help and support. Research has shown social skills impairments in children diagnosed with conduct disorders, mood disorders, anxiety disorders, autism spectrum disorders, attention-deficit/hyperactivity disorder (ADHD), learning disabilities, and other behavioral challenges (Rutherford et al., 2004).

Typical deficits include difficulty initiating and responding in social interactions, making and maintaining eye contact, reading non-verbal cues (including facial expressions and body language), taking another person's perspective, recognizing feelings, and knowing what to talk about and for how long.

Consequences of Social Skills Impairments

When supported learning opportunities are not provided, the lack of positive peer interactions can lead to avoidance of social opportunities and a downward spiral, as fewer opportunities for learning are encountered. This makes it difficult for a child to develop and maintain meaningful personal relationships. Often, as a result, these children gravitate towards solitary play and activities.

Teaching Social Skills

Finding ways and opportunities to practice social interaction skills in a supportive environment can be difficult. However, while not as straightforward to teach as, for example, multiplication facts, social skills <u>can</u> be taught and strengthened. Children with special learning needs may require intentional instruction that can include modeling, role playing social scenarios, social stories, and instruction based on the techniques and principles of Applied Behavior Analysis.

What Is Applied Behavior Analysis?

Conceptual Foundation

Based on learning theory (Skinner, 1953), Applied Behavior Analysis (ABA) is a scientific approach for teaching new skills and decreasing behaviors that are harmful or interfere with learning.

Because of its scientific foundation, ABA focuses on measurable behavior change that is the result of events that occur before and/or after a behavior (Baer et al, 1968). Events that occur after a behavior and increase its likelihood of reoccurring are called reinforcers. On the other hand, punishment after a behavior decreases the likelihood it will occur again.

Teaching Strategies

ABA Practitioners (Board Certified Behavior Analysts or BCBAs) use many different teaching strategies. These include specific instructional techniques, such as direct instruction and discrete trial training. "Shaping," the process of teaching closer and closer approximations to the desired skill, is a commonly used technique. Another is "chaining," in which smaller skills are learned and linked together to accomplish a larger task.

However, ABA is not a "one size fits all" approach; because the needs for each child are different, the goals and strategies used to achieve them are individually tailored for each child. Progress is continuously measured and modifications to goals and strategies are based on the measured outcomes, resulting in efficient and effective treatment.

Goals

ABA has been used to help improve the lives of individuals by focusing on behaviors that are socially significant for the individual. A wide variety of different skills, such as communication & language skills, academics, self-help skills, work skills, domestic and life skills, self-monitoring, play skills, and social skills have been taught using ABA strategies. ABA principles have also been used to help decrease problematic behaviors, such as self-injury and aggression. In all cases, the goal is to bring about meaningful and positive behavior change.

Overview of the Green Box Kids Social Skills Curriculum

Developed by a team of BCBAs and professional artists, the Green Box Kids Social Skills Curriculum and supplemental materials support a comprehensive approach to social skills training. Although the curriculum evolved from application of principles of behavior analysis, no special training in ABA is necessary to use the materials. Our mission is to provide professionals, including speech and language pathologists, special educators, psychologists, counselors, and applied behavior analysts with engaging tools that are inherently motivating for learners. Additionally, we aim to provide parents with the tools they need to address social skills challenges, even if they cannot access private therapy on their own.

Relatable Characters

The Green Box Kids Social Skills Curriculum offers a unique approach to social skills lessons by introducing relatable characters that are easy for children to connect with. The Green Box Kids are a group of elementary school-aged friends who deal with the kinds of social skills challenges that many students regularly encounter. Each of the kids has unique likes, dislikes, strengths, and challenges that define them. As learners get to know each character, they may find themselves relating to their favorite Green Box Kids' quirks and idiosyncrasies. Just like regular kids, the Green Box Kids are not perfect.

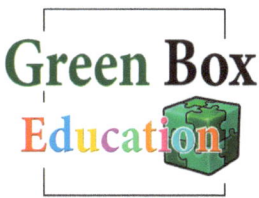

Realistic Scenarios in Comic Book Format

The art in the Green Box Kids curriculum is presented in a comic book format. Unlike other popular materials, the lessons contain minimal text, which allows learners to easily navigate social lessons without being burdened with unnecessary language. Because the kids look and act like real kids participating in real life scenarios, students have the opportunity to observe and reflect on realistic facial expressions and body language, which are critical building blocks to social development.

Active Responding and Practice

Through active responding and practice, the activities in the book create opportunities for new skills to be acquired and strengthened in a supported environment that promotes successful social interactions. Real world social interactions are often complex, unpredictable, and varied. To reflect this, an answer key is not included for these activities, leaving flexibility for answers based on the varied, but appropriate, ways to react to a social situation.

Meet the Kids! Cami, Mei, Lucy, Tito, Barry, Richard, Jack, and Lisa

About This Volume

Flexibility

In each of the three social comics and lessons in this volume, the Green Box Kids learn more about what it means to **be flexible** and why it is important. Flexibility with outcomes is a vital life and social skill that children need to learn in order to make and keep friends and in a social setting, such as a classroom. While being flexible can be a challenge, it can be learned and developed with practice and support.

Being flexible means being able to react appropriately in the presence of changing situations. The lessons in this volume help children learn how to react during situations involving changes in routine or schedule, unexpected events/actions of others, and uncertain outcomes. Some strategies for calming down when frustration does occur are also included. Importantly, the comics show the reactions of all of the people involved in the social interaction to show how the actions of each Green Box Kids affects their friendships. The supporting activities walk your learner though the concept of flexibility as they compare what they are learning to what happens to their favorite Green Box Kids characters.

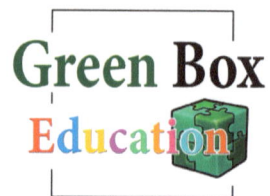

How To Use This Book

The Green Box Kids Social Skills Curriculum is ideally used in a group setting with similar-aged peers and/or other children at a comparable developmental level. Group settings provide opportunities for discussion, sharing of ideas and real-life scenarios, and active practice of the skills. However, the materials can be used individually, for example, in the home, with the parent filling the role of the social "peer."

Each lesson focuses on a different component of the social skill. However, all of the lessons are set-up in the same format. Each lesson consists of:

Warm-Up Questions

Each lesson starts with a series of "warm-up" questions about the topic. Use these questions to find out how much the learner already knows about the topic that will be covered. These questions introduce the topic and will be answered in the course of the lesson, so you don't need to spend too much time discussing them.

The Comic

In 6 – 7 panels, the comic sets up a socially-based problem and an "inappropriate" solution to the problem.

Breakdown of Comic, Panel By Panel

The comic is broken down, panel by panel, with 1 – 2 questions that encourage the learner to concentrate on social cues (facial expressions, body language) for clues. This facilitates conversation about and engagement with the characters' feelings and reactions.

Follow-up Questions

A series of follow-up questions are included to check comprehension of the events and concepts presented in the comic.

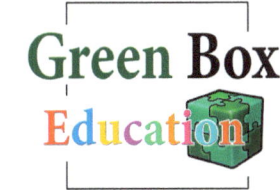

Learning Activities

Two to three learning activities, presented in a variety of learning formats, provide practice with the social concepts. Many of the activities are designed to be completed with a partner or group, opening the door for application and practice of the skill.

Solution Comic & Wrap-up Discussion

Each lesson ends with an opportunity for the learner to draw a comic panel with a guess about a solution to the social problem. An appropriate solution comic is then presented, along with 1 or 2 questions designed to wrap-up the lesson. You may also go back and ask the Warm-up Questions again to see how much the student has learned.

Tips

- Use social praise for appropriate responses and interactions.
- Although space has been provided for written answers, learners may either write in their own answers or give them verbally, depending on skill level.
- If used in a group, as the adult you should be sure to function as a discussion leader
    - Encourage the group to go beyond just answering the question and to "dig deeper"
    - During the discussion, relate the answers to real-life examples
    - Don't let the discussion get off-topic
    - Don't let one or two kids dominate the discussion
    - Find ways to involve everyone in the group discussion and activities
- Provide guidance and prompts/suggestions, as needed. But encourage peer facilitation.
- Whenever possible, find ways during the lessons to provide opportunities to practice the skill in the social group setting.

How To Measure Progress

Measuring progress is an essential component of any curriculum. Below is guidance for measuring progress. For parents or educators with little to no experience in Applied Behavior Analysis (ABA), we have included a straightforward and easy way to measure development of skills (Appendix A). Progress in the school setting can be measured by including a flexibility goal on the child's Individualized Education Program (IEP). Some suggested IEP goals can be found in Appendix B. For ABA professionals and educators with more experience in ABA, a more detailed behavior change program is outlined in Appendix C.

Let's say that you want to know if a child is making progress in learning math facts. A common assessment method is the "speed drill," in which the child is given one minute to complete a worksheet with one hundred math problems. It is not unusual to administer a speed drill before any instruction begins (a "pretest", in order to determine how much the child already knows. The speed drill may be given weekly, until the child receives a particular score (for example, at least 90 correct out of 100).

Measuring progress made while learning social skills is a bit more complex but conceptually the same. There are two things that you will need to decide: (1) what to measure and (2) when to measure.

What to Measure

Progress should be shown not only in how a learner answers the questions in this book but also in development of overall skills. We recommend using the materials found in Appendix A to assess overall skill development. The rating scale and checklist help determine how flexible the child is during situations when unexpected things happen, when a nonpreferred outcome cannot be changed, and when there is uncertainty about how a situation with resolve.

When to Measure

As with the speed drills, it is best to first determine what the child already knows or can do. Therefore, we recommend assessing the current skill level before you begin using the materials. Then, after the book has been completed, assess how much the child has learned. Because each of the lessons in this book focus on a different component of the social skill, you could do a learning check after each lesson, similar to administering speed drills once a week.

Summary and Extension

After this book has been completed, the learner should have a greater understanding of the targeted social skill and the ways in which it is important for developing and maintaining relationships with others. Additionally, the child will have learned some strategies related to displaying the skill. However, social skill development is a process and you should continue to provide opportunities for practice. Children who are still developing foundational social skills often feel more comfortable in small groups. Regardless of the group size, try to make the environment comfortable and supportive, while providing feedback, guidance, and praise for appropriate behaviors. Finally, don't forget that adult behavior can provide a good example of how to respond to social situations, so find and use opportunities to model appropriate responses.

References

Baer, D.M., Wolf, M.M., & Risley, T.R., (1968). Some current dimensions of applied behavior analysis. *Journal of Applied Behavior Analysis*, 1, 91-97.

Rutherford, R.B.Jr., Quinn, M.M., & Mathur, S.R. (2004). Handbook of Research in Emotional and Behavioral Disorders. New York, NY: The Guilford Press.

Skinner, B.F. (1953). Science and Human Behavior. New York, NY: The MacMillian Press.

Let's Learn About Flexibility
Lesson 1: Traffic

Find out what you already know about being flexible.

1. Why do people feel angry when something frustrating happens?
___
___
___

2. Why do people feel angry *with others* when something frustrating happens?
___
___
___

3. How do you feel when someone yells at you for something that isn't your fault?
___
___
___

4. What are some things you can do when you feel frustrated?
___
___
___

5. What are some ways to tell someone that you are frustrated or disappointed?
___
___
___

Lesson 1: Traffic

Read the comic on the following page about Jack and his Mom to learn about a time when something frustrating happened. Make sure to look closely at the faces to see how they may be feeling.

Let's Break It Down!

Now we are going to break the comic down to get a better idea of what is going on in each picture.

What are Jack and his mom doing?

What do you see in this picture?

What is Jack's facial expression?

Does she look happy, angry, or neutral?

Talk about Jack and his mom's body language.

Why is Jack's mouth open wide?

Let's Think About It!

The questions on the following page will help us better understand the comic we just read.

Answer the following questions about the comic you just read. Some questions may have more than one right answer.

1. Why is Jack going to be late?
   _____
   _____
   _____

2. What/who does Jack blame?
   _____
   _____
   _____

3. Do we know what caused the traffic jam? Was it Jack's mom?
   _____
   _____
   _____

4. How do you think Jack's mom felt about the traffic jam?
   _____
   _____
   _____

5. What can Jack's mom do to get him there on time?
   _____
   _____
   _____

6. Did Jack notice how his mom is feeling about the traffic jam?

___

7. Why did Jack get mad at his mom?

___

8. Jack was mad at his mom for something that wasn't her fault. How do you think this made her feel?

___

9. Do you think Jack's friends will be mad at him for being late?

___

10. If he explains why he is late, do you think they will still be his friend?

___

Whatever Happens, Happens.

In this next section we will talk about things we can do when something happens that we can't change.

Talk about it with your friends!

Talk about a time when you felt frustrated when something unexpected happened.

Talk about a time when you felt angry about an outcome that you couldn't change.

Partner up with a friend and come up with ideas for 2 other ways Jack could have acted and the pros and cons of each. Be sure to think about how Jack and his mom would feel!

Idea #1: _____

PROS	**CONS**

Idea #2: _____

PROS	**CONS**

Now, which one do you think is the BEST solution? Talk about it with your partner and write your answer here:

In our comic, Jack got frustrated and angry because something happened that he couldn't change. Here are some things that might happen to you.

Can You Change It?

	YES, I can!	NOPE
My friend bought me socks for my birthday.	☐	☐
My favorite video game is Mario Kart®.	☐	☐
There are 50 questions on the math quiz.	☐	☐
It is raining today.	☐	☐
I am practicing free throws during free time.	☐	☐
I am yelling at my mom.	☐	☐
The toy store is closed when we get there.	☐	☐
My best friend doesn't sit next to me in class.	☐	☐

With a partner, think of some other things that you can and can't change.

Yes, I can change it:

_____
_____
_____

Nope, I can't change it:

_____
_____
_____

Let's See What We Learned!

Let's go back to the original comic. Look it over one more time and come up with an idea for what you think Jack should do.

What do you think should happen next?

Draw what you think Jack should do:

Let's See What The Green Box Kids Came Up With!

Jack lets his Mom know why he is frustrated.

Talk with your friends about their solutions.

Let's Learn About Flexibility
Lesson 2: The Party

Find out what you already know about being flexible.

1. Are there things that happen that you can't change? Give an example.
___
___
___

2. How do you feel when you are worried about something?
___
___
___

3. What can you do if a friend is worried about something?
___
___
___

4. Give an example of a way to tell a friend that you are worried about something.
___
___
___

5. How do you feel if you try to help a friend and he isn't listening? Explain.
___
___
___

Lesson 2: The Party

Read the comic on the following page about Lisa and Lucy to learn about a time when Lucy was worried and anxious. Make sure to look closely at the Green Box Kids' faces to see how they may be feeling.

Let's Break It Down!

Now we are going to break the comic down to get a better idea of what is going on in each picture.

What is going on in this picture?

Look at Lucy's eyes and eyebrows. How are they different from the last picture?

Describe Lucy's facial expression.

What is the difference between Lucy's facial expression and Lisa's facial expression?

How has Lisa's body language changed?

How do both girls feel?

Let's Think About It!

The questions on the following page will help us better understand the comic we just read.

Answer the following questions about the comic you just read. Some questions may have more than one right answer.

1. What makes a party fun? Do friends help make a party fun?
   _____
   _____
   _____

2. Why did Lucy think her party wouldn't be fun?
   _____
   _____
   _____

3. Did Lisa think the party would be fun? How do you know?
   _____
   _____
   _____

4. How did Lisa try to help Lucy feel better and not worry?
   _____
   _____
   _____

5. What are some things that Lisa might have been thinking and feeling?
   _____
   _____
   _____

6. Do you think Lisa is going to have fun at the party?

_____

_____

_____

7. Here are some reasons why Lucy's friends might not make it to the party.

	Will it happen?	Can she change it?
Got lost	Yes No Maybe	Yes No Maybe
Got sick	Yes No Maybe	Yes No Maybe
Changed their minds	Yes No Maybe	Yes No Maybe
Traffic jam	Yes No Maybe	Yes No Maybe

8. Do you think Lucy should worry so much about things she can't change? _____

9. What can Lucy do to stop herself from worrying?

_____

_____

_____

10. Do you think Lucy is going to have fun at her party? Why?

_____

_____

_____

But What If…?

Sometimes, when we really want something to happen the way we are hoping and planning, it is hard not to worry about what will happen. In this section we will talk about what makes us worried and what we could do.

Talk about it with your friends!

Talk with your friends about a time when you were really looking forward to something and it turned out the way you hoped it would.

Talk with your friends about a time when you were really looking forward to something and it DID NOT turn out the way you hoped it would.

Lisa was frustrated because Lucy wouldn't listen when she tried to help. With a partner, come up with two other ways LISA could have acted and the pros and cons of each. Be sure to think about how Lucy and Lisa would feel!

Idea #1: _____

PROS	CONS

Idea #2: _____

PROS	CONS

Now, which one do you think is the BEST solution? Talk about it with your partner and write your answer here:

Lucy was worried because she didn't know whether her friends were coming to her party. Here are some things that might happen. How sure are you that they will happen.

My family will have pizza for dinner. I am

Very sure				Kinda sure				Not sure
|-------|-------|-------|-------|-------|-------|

The class will have indoor recess if it is raining. I am

Very sure				Kinda sure				Not sure
|-------|-------|-------|-------|-------|-------|

The teacher will give us homework on Friday. I am

Very sure				Kinda sure				Not sure
|-------|-------|-------|-------|-------|-------|

I will be late for school if I miss the bus. I am

Very sure				Kinda sure				Not sure
|-------|-------|-------|-------|-------|-------|

The car will stop if it runs out of gas. I am

Very sure				Kinda sure				Not sure
|-------|-------|-------|-------|-------|-------|

It the glass falls on the floor, it will break. I am

Very sure				Kinda sure				Not sure
|-------|-------|-------|-------|-------|-------|

Let's See What We Learned!

Let's go back to the original comic. Look it over one more time and come up with an idea for what you think the Green Box Kids should do.

What do you think should happen next?

Draw what you think the Kids should do:

Let's See What The Green Box Kids Came Up With!

Lisa reassures Lucy and she stops worrying.

Do you think that Lucy and Lisa will have fun at the party? Why? Talk with your friends.

Let's Learn About Flexibility
Lesson 3: The Test

Find out what you already know about being flexible.

1. Give an example of when you were worried about how things would turn out?
   _____
   _____
   _____

2. Does worrying about something change what will happen?
   _____
   _____
   _____

3. What are some good ways to calm down when you are upset?
   _____
   _____
   _____

4. How do you feel when a friend keeps interrupting you?
   _____
   _____
   _____

5. Do you like to hang out with friends who worry a lot?
   _____
   _____
   _____

Lesson 3: The Test

Read the comic on the following page about Lisa and Barry to learn about a time when Lisa was worried and anxious. Make sure to look closely at the Green Box Kids' faces to see how they may be feeling.

Let's Break It Down!

Now we are going to break the comic down to get a better idea of what is going on in each picture.

What are Lisa and Barry doing?

How does Lisa feel in this picture?

What is Barry trying to do in this picture?

Is Lisa looking at Barry?

What do notice about Lisa's body language in this picture?

Do Barry's eyes look happy? How can you tell?

Let's Think About It!

The questions on the following page will help us better understand the comic we just read.

Answer the following questions about the comic you just read. Some questions may have more than one right answer.

1. Does Lisa know if Barry is worried about his grade? How do you know?

_____
_____
_____

2. How do you feel when a friend doesn't let you finish talking?

_____
_____
_____

3. How did it make Barry feel?

_____
_____
_____

4. What is Lisa worried about?

_____
_____
_____

5. Why is it so hard for Lisa to stop worrying about her grade?

_____
_____
_____

6. Does Lisa's future depend on this test grade?

_____
_____
_____

7. What do you think could happen if Lisa gets a "C" on the test?

	Will it happen?
Her parents make her move out	Yes No Maybe
She will ask for help preparing for the next test	Yes No Maybe
She will do the extra credit math assignment	Yes No Maybe
She will not be able to go to college	Yes No Maybe

8. Is there anything Lisa can do to change her test grade?

_____
_____
_____

9. Is there anything Barry could have done to help her feel better?

_____
_____
_____

10. Can Lisa and Barry still be friends? Why?

_____
_____
_____

No worries.

Not knowing how something is going to turn out can make us feel worried and anxious. In this section, we are going to talk about some ways that we can stay calm and feel less worried.

Talk about it with your friends!

Talk with your friends about a time when you were really worried about how things would turn out.

What does it feel like when you are worried?

Partner up with a friend and come up with ideas for 2 other ways Lisa could have acted and the pros and cons of each. Be sure to think about how Lisa and Barry would feel!

Idea #1: _____

PROS	CONS

Idea #2: _____

PROS	CONS

Now, which one do you think is the BEST solution? Talk about it with your partner and write your answer here:

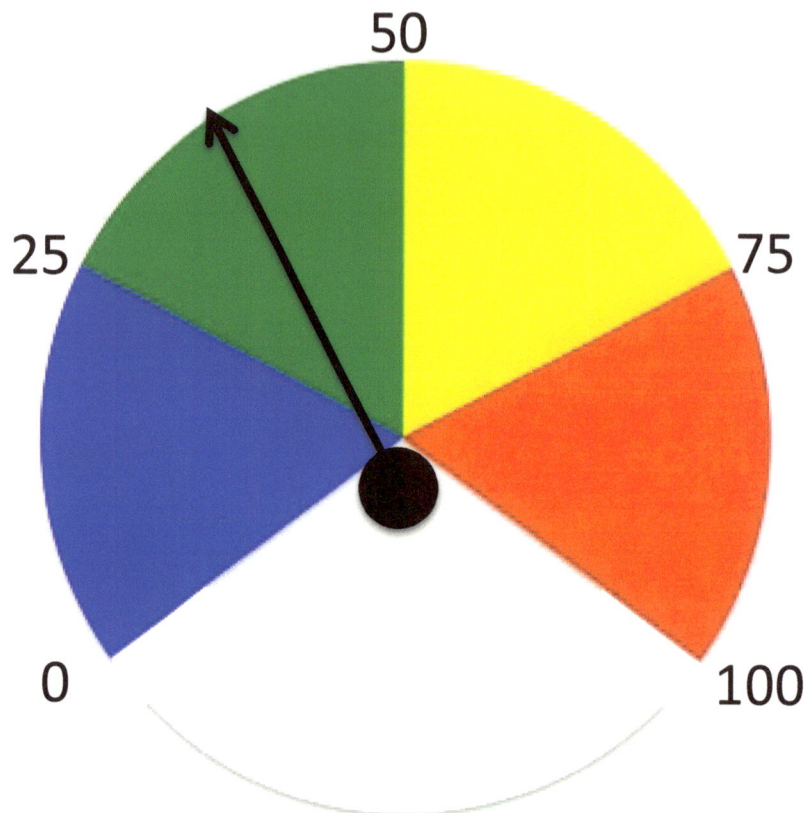

There are different ways we can think about how we feel. Sometimes it helps to use colors, temperature, or speed.

BLUE: cold /slow. When you are "blue" you might feel sad or bored or low energy (moving too slow)

GREEN: just right: When you are "green" you might feel happy, calm, moving at just the right speed

YELLOW: heating up/speeding up. When you are "yellow" things are heating up/speeding up. You might feel frustrated, worried, anxious, or like you are going to get angry.

RED: hot/too fast: When you are "red" you might feel angry or out of control.

Sometimes, when we are feeling YELLOW (worried/frustrated) or RED (angry), it is hard to stay calm. Next, we are going to practice some things that can help. After you and your partner try each one, share if you liked it.

	Liked it!	Didn't like it.
Take a **deep breath**. Hold your breath and count to 5. Breathe out slowly.	☐	☐
Close your eyes. Imagine someplace that is calm and peaceful. Stay quiet and think about your calm place.	☐	☐
Make a tight fist. Count to 3. Wiggle your fingers to **relax** your muscles as you count to 3. Do it again.	☐	☐
Stretch your arms over head. Count to 5. Stretch your arms to the side. Count to 5. Stretch them down to the floor. Count to 5.	☐	☐
Rub your hands together very **fast** while you count to 5. Now rub your hands together very **slowly** while you count to 5.	☐	☐

Which one did you like the best? Tell your partner why you liked it.

With your partner, think of some other things that can help you stay calm when you are feeling YELLOW or RED.

_____
_____
_____

Let's See What We Learned!

Let's go back to the original comic. Look it over one more time and come up with an idea for what you think the Green Box Kids should do.

What do you think should happen next?

Draw what you think the Kids should do:

Let's See What The Green Box Kids Came Up With!

Lisa calmed down and stopped interrupting.

What color do you think Lisa is feeling? What things do you think she did to calm down?

Appendix A: Measuring Progress

Flexibility Pre-Test

Before you begin using the lessons, use this pre-test to determine the child's current skill level.

The scales below describe different kinds of flexibility skills. Rate HOW OFTEN the child engages in each behavior without any adult assistance. Base your ratings on recent observations.

Recognizes situations that are out of his/her control (*Things that cannot be changed, things that are unexpected, etc.*):

Remains calm when something unexpected happens (*Uses calm and appropriate language, does not cry, etc*):

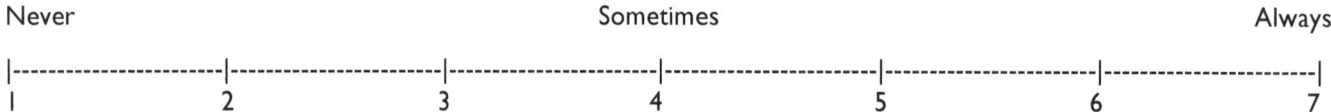

Remains calm when there is uncertainty about a future outcome (*Uses calm and appropriate language, does not cry, etc*):

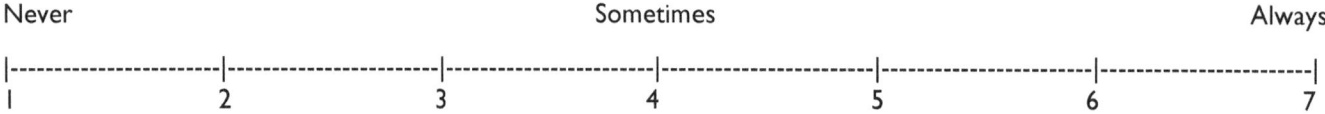

Remains calm when an outcome cannot be changed (*Uses calm and appropriate language, does not cry, etc*):

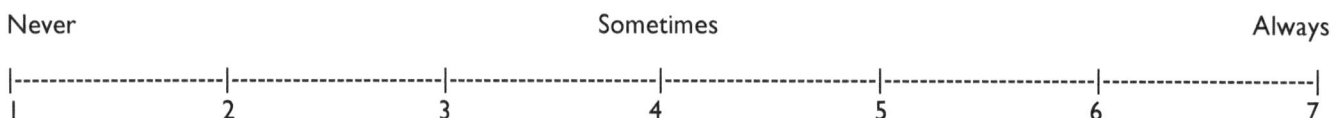

Can identify appropriate calming strategies to use when frustrated (*Calm breathing, counting to 10, etc.*):

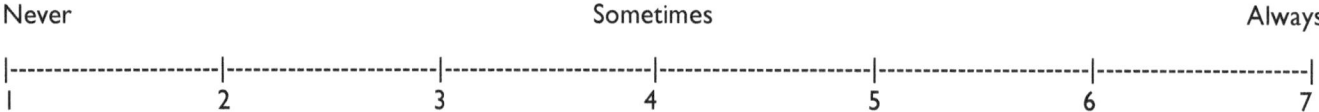

Flexibility Behavior Checklist

After you have completed the pretest, use this form to track development of flexibility skills while using the lessons.

Instructions:

- Whenever you notice the child presented with an opportunity to be flexible use the form on the next page to:
    - Record the date.
    - Make notes about the activity. This could include the setting, who is present and/or how many other children are present, as well as what activities they are engaged in.
    - In the Skill section, make a checkmark in the box that most accurately describes the skill being displayed (note that these are also the skills assessed in the pretest).
    - In the Child's Response section, make a checkmark in the box that most accurately describe the way that the child responded.
        - Independently: Responded correctly without any adult assistance
        - Prompted: Responded correctly with adult assistance
        - Did not occur: A correct response did not occur
        - Problem Behavior: Some problem behavior occurred in response (for example, child tantrums when an unexpected outcome occurs).

Where to track skills:

- If you are using the lessons in a group format, use the form on the following page to track skills displayed in that setting.
- Other settings in which you can track skills:
    - Classroom
    - Home
    - Social groups (scout meetings, teams, clubs, etc.)

Measuring Progress:

- The goal is for the child to respond more frequently without adult assistance.
- If you are working with an ABA or other professional, you can share this information with them.

Extension:

You may continue to track the development of flexibility skills after you have completed the lessons using this form.

Flexibility Behavior Checklist

Date	Activity	Skill (check one)					Child's Response (check one)			
		Recognizes situations that are out of his/her child's control	Remains calm when something unexpected happens	Remains calm when there is uncertainty about a future outcome	Remains calm when an outcome cannot be changed	Can identify appropriate calming strategies to use when frustrated	Independently	Prompted	Did not Occur	Problem Behavior

Flexibility Post-Test

After finishing the lessons, use this post-test to determine the child's current skill level. DO NOT REVIEW THE PRE-TEST SCORES!

The scales below describe different kinds of flexibility skills. Rate HOW OFTEN the child engages in each behavior without any adult assistance. Base your ratings on current behavior only.

Recognizes situations that are out of his/her control (*Things that cannot be changed, things that are unexpected, etc.*):

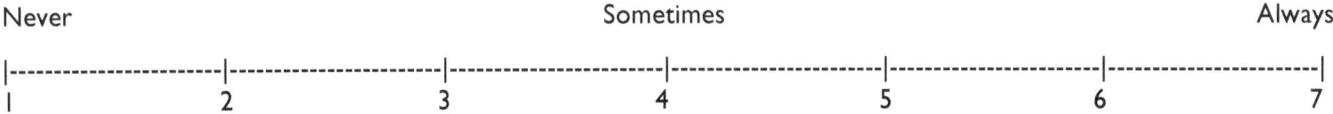

Remains calm when something unexpected happens (*Uses calm and appropriate language, does not cry, etc*):

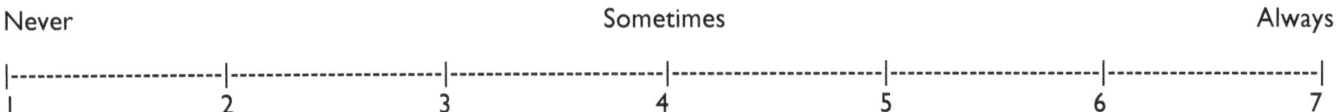

Remains calm when there is uncertainty about a future outcome (*Uses calm and appropriate language, does not cry, etc*):

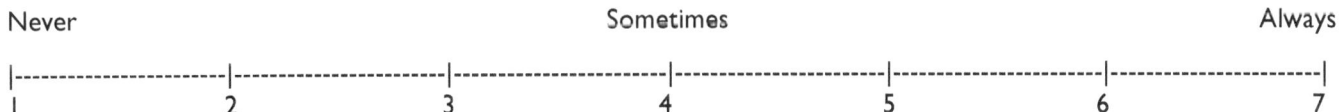

Remains calm when an outcome cannot be changed (*Uses calm and appropriate language, does not cry, etc*):

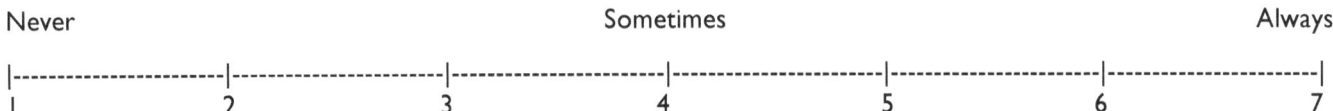

Can identify appropriate calming strategies to use when frustrated (*Calm breathing, counting to 10, etc.*):

Pre-Post Comparison

- Fill in the chart below to compare flexibility skills before and after using the lessons.

- To determine the degree of change (Change Score), subtract the pre-test score from the post-test score.

- For each item on the scale, more appropriate responses receive higher valued scores. Any change scores that are greater than 1, indicate that you have seen a change in that skill.

- Any skills that were scored lower on the Post-Test than the Pre-Test may need additional training. However, it is also possible that after using both the lessons and Flexibility Checklist you are a more keen observer than before. This increased awareness to the types of responses the child is making may account for lower scores.
    - Compare the progress on the Flexibility Checklist with the scores.
        - If the child is showing progress (more independent responses) on the Checklist, then progress is being made.
        - If the child is not showing progress on the Checklist, then additional learning opportunities and direct teaching is needed.

Skill	Pre-Test Score	Post-Test Score	Change (Post-test minus Pre-test) Score
Recognizes situations that are out of his/her control			
Remains calm when something unexpected happens			
Remains calm when there is uncertainty about a future outcome			
Remains calm when an outcome cannot be changed			
Can identify appropriate calming strategies to use when frustrated			

Notes:

Appendix B: Individualized Education Program Goals

Individualized Education Program Goals

The Individualized Education Program (IEP) is a document that defines the individualized objectives of a child who has been determined to have a disability that will impact their ability to receive an appropriate public education. Each IEP is tailored to meet the individual students' needs, as determined by evaluation (assessments and evaluations by school psychologists, standardized tests, performance on academic tasks, etc.). To meet those needs, the IEP includes measurable annual goals addressing each area of need.

As you have learned through these materials, flexibility is a complex social skill that involves means being able to react appropriately in the presence of changing situations, such situations involving changes in routine or schedule, unexpected events/actions of others, and uncertain outcomes.

Below are several suggested flexibility goals. A good goal is one that is individualized for the student, reflects the student's current level of performance, and is a reasonable expectation for improvement over the course of the IEP year.

Sample Flexibility Goal #1:
When denied access to a preferred object, activity, or food, will exhibit appropriate behavior on _____ out of ___ opportunities for _____ consecutive days, as measured by teacher/staff data and observation.

Sample Flexibility Goal #2:
With fading prompts and supports, will exhibit appropriate behavior during daily transitions on _____ out of _____ opportunities for _____ consecutive days, as measured by teacher/staff data and observation.

Sample Flexibility Goal #3:
When presented with scenarios concerning flexibility, will identify appropriate solutions on _____ out of _____ opportunities for _____ consecutive days, as measured by teacher/staff data and observation.

Notes:

Appendix C: For the ABA Professional

Flexibility

Use the materials in this book as a part of a comprehensive approach to teaching appropriate flexibility skills.

Purpose: Increasing flexibility strategies while decreasing maladaptive behaviors in contrived social scenarios.

Procedure:

The following are potential behaviors and goals. Successfully implemented Applied Behavior Analysis (ABA) therapy is individualized; specific behaviors and goals should be determined for each student. Remember, goals should be clear, concise, and easy to objectively track.

1. Define **behaviors** for each learner (use the data sheet on the following page). Examples (will vary on a learner by learner basis):
    a. "Identification of flexibility solution" is defined as independently identifying an appropriate reaction to a flexibility scenario
    b. Tantrum behavior is defined as hitting, kicking, screaming, or eloping when an unexpected outcome occurs.
2. Define **goals** for each learner for each behavior (use the data sheet on the following page). Examples:
    a. Flexibility: Student A will suggest a minimum of 2 solutions to a flexibility scenario as defined in the target.
    b. Tantrum: Student A will exhibit 0 tantrum episodes across 3 consecutive social scenarios for a given target.
3. Determine **targets** for each learner (use data sheet on the following page).
    a. Reduce the skill/behavior into smaller elements.
4. Use appropriate ABA procedures, such as prompts and prompt fading, errorless teaching, etc., to teach individual elements.
5. Use reinforcement to strengthen each new element.
6. Continue presenting opportunities until the learner(s) have mastered the goal at that target. We recommend continuing a target until the learner responds correctly on at least 80% of the opportunities for several consecutive sessions.
7. Use the suggested activities below to contrive opportunities to work on the targets.

"Delayed" Activity – While engaged in a neutral task (for example, a work activity), inform the students that access to a preferred activity (for example, a video game) will be available after a specified amount of time (5 minutes, etc.). At or near the end of the time, inform the students that the activity is not available (for example, "the TV isn't working, I need to fix it"). As the students demonstrate skill in waiting without problem behavior, increase the length of the delay or begin delaying highly preferred activities.
"Unexpected" Activity – Provide the students with a schedule of tasks. As one of those tasks is drawing to a close, inform the students that there has been a change in the schedule. Either rearrange the order of the remaining tasks or substitute a different task for one of them. To make the activity more difficult use a non-preferred task as the unexpected activity.
"Uncertain" Activity – Provide the students with a schedule of tasks. Make, and display, a list of student suggestions for a final, preferred task. Tell the students that if there is time at the end you will select one of those tasks.

Student: _____

Behavioral Definitions and Goal(s):

Behavior	Definition	Goal

Target	Date Target Introduced	Date Target Mastered

About The Authors

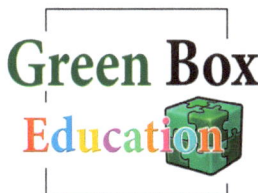

Carl Dzyak, M.Ed. (Special Education, George Mason University), BCBA, LBA is the founder and CEO of Green Box ABA. He founded Green Box ABA, PLLC in October 2014. Carl has been a practicing behavior analyst since 2011 and has worked with individuals on the autism spectrum since 2007.

Barbara Kaminski, Ph.D (Psychology/Behavior Analysis, West Virginia University), BCBA-D, LBA is the ABA Clinical Director at Green Box ABA, PLLC. She teaches graduate level courses in ABA for both George Mason University and The Chicago School of Professional Psychology and maintains an Adjunct Faculty appointment at The Johns Hopkins University School of Medicine Department of Psychiatry and Behavioral Sciences. Dr. Kaminski has been working in clinical practice since 2013 and in the broader field of behavior analysis for over 20 years.

Chris Richardson, M.Ed. (Special Education, George Mason University), BCBA, LBA is COO of Green Box ABA, PLLC. He has been working in Applied Behavior Analysis since 2012 and has worked with children with special needs since 2007.

About The Artist

Sarah Miller began her art career with Game Design and Animation studies at The Art Institute of Washington, and later ended at George Mason University where she earned her Bachelor's of Individualized Study in Visual Arts and Narrative. She is a digital artist and game designer with a passion for creating, no matter its medium —there is nothing she loves more than bringing characters and worlds to life, "bridging connections between people with art and inspiration."

About Green Box ABA, PLLC

Green Box ABA, PLLC is an Applied Behavior Analysis (ABA) clinic located in Springfield, Virginia that provides innovative Applied Behavior Analysis therapy and high quality resources to clients seeking meaningful behavioral change. The therapy is rooted in science, but the approach is rooted in compassion.

www.ingramcontent.com/pod-product-compliance
Lightning Source LLC
Chambersburg PA
CBHW042032150426
43200CB00002B/23